# IF YOU KNOW YOU KNOW 90'S - 00'S HIPHOP AND R&B TRIVIA BOOK

Bakes Books

Hip hop and R&B reached new heights of mainstream success and cultural relevance in the 90's - 00'S thanks to an unheard-of rise in popularity. Artists like Boyz II Men, The Notorious B.I.G., Aaliyah, TLC, and Tupac Shakur became well-known, topping the charts and enthralling listeners with their distinctive fusion of soulful melodies, gritty lyrics, and addictive beats. Rap's emergence as a major force in popular music, as well as the period's distinctive musical style and fashion movements, all served to define this time period.

Welcome to the ultimate journey through the greatest era of hip hop and R&B - the vibrant and influential time. This trivia book is a nostalgic flash back to the iconic artists, memorable songs, and groundbreaking moments that defined a 2 decades in music history. Whether you're an Old Head, a curious newcomer, or someone longing to relive the glory days, get ready to test your knowledge and immerse yourself in the rich tapestry of hip hop and R&B.

1. In the 1993 hit song "Gin and juice" by Dr. Dre and Snoop Dogg, what does Snoop Dogg say he has on his mind?
   A) His money
   B) Women and money
   C) Fast cars and fame

2. Which hip hop artist released the album "The Chronic" in 1992?
   A) 2Pac
   B) Notorious B.I.G.
   C) Dr. Dre

3. Finish this lyric from TLC's 1995 hit "Waterfalls": "Don't go chasing..."
   A) Rainbows
   B) Dreams
   C) Waterfalls

1) Answer: A) His money
2) Answer: C) Dr. Dre
3) Answer: C) Waterfalls

4. What was the title of Aaliyah's debut album released in 1994?
   A) "Age Ain't Nothing but a Number"
   B) "One in a Million"
   C) "Aaliyah"

5. Who was one of the original group members of Destiny's Child in the 90s?
   A) LaTavia Roberson
   B) Toni Braxton
   C) Michelle Williams

6. Which hip hop duo had a hit with the song "Regulate" in 1994?
   A) OutKast
   B) Gang Starr
   C) Warren G and Nate Dogg

4) Answer: A) "Age Ain't Nothing but a Number"
5) Answer: A) LaTavia Roberson
6) Answer: C) Warren G and Nate Dogg

7. What is the real name of the rapper known as Notorious B.I.G.?
   A) Sean Combs
   B) Christopher Wallace
   C) Jay-Z

8. Which artist released the album "My Life" in 1994?
   A) Mary J. Blige
   B) Lauryn Hill
   C) Erykah Badu

9. Finish this lyric from Snoop Dogg's 1993 hit "Gin and Juice": "Rollin' down the street..."
   A) In my '64
   B) With my homies
   C) Smokin' indo

7) Answer: B) Christopher Wallace
8) Answer: A) Mary J. Blige
9) Answer: C) Smokin' indo

10. What was the title of 2Pac's debut solo album released in 1991?
    A) "All Eyez on Me"
    B) "Me Against the World"
    C) "2Pacalypse Now"


11. Which R&B group released the song "No Diggity" in 1996?
    A) Boyz II Men
    B) Jodeci
    C) Blackstreet


12. Who released the hit single "Fantasy" in 1995?
    A) Mariah Carey
    B) Whitney Houston
    C) Janet Jackson

10) Answer: C) "2Pacalypse Now"
11) Answer: C) Blackstreet
12) Answer: A) Mariah Carey

13. What was the name of the female rapper who released the album "Hard Core" in 1996?
    A) Lil' Kim
    B) Missy Elliott
    C) Foxy Brown


14. Finish this lyric from Wu-Tang Clan's 1993 hit "C.R.E.A.M.": "Cash rules everything..."
    A) Around me
    B) In this world
    C) In my pocket


15. Which hip hop group released the album "The Score" in 1996?
    A) Public Enemy
    B) N.W.A.
    C) The Fugees


13) Answer: A) Lil' Kim
14) Answer: A) Around me
15) Answer: C) The Fugees

16. Who released the album "CrazySexyCool" in 1994?
   A) TLC
   B) Salt-N-Pepa
   C) En Vogue

17. Finish this lyric from Montell Jordan's 1995 hit "This Is How We Do It": "I gotta get mine in a big black truck..."
   A) Party and have a good time
   B) You can get yours in a '64
   C) The party's underway

18. Name R&B singer Jon B's 1995 debut album?
   A) The Score
   B) are you still down
   C) Bonafide

16) Answer: A) TLC
17) Answer: B) You can get yours in a '64
18) Answer: C) Bonafide

19. Who sang the hook on Warren G's 1994 hit "Regulate"?
   A) Nate Dogg
   B) Snoop Dogg
   C) Dr. Dre

20. Which hip hop artist released the song "Gangsta's Paradise" in 1995?
   A) Coolio
   B) Ice Cube
   C) Snoop Dogg

21. What was the title of Jay-Z's debut album released in 1996?
   A) "The Blueprint"
   B) "Reasonable Doubt"
   C) "Vol. 2... Hard Knock Life"

19) Answer: A) Nate Dogg
20) Answer: A) Coolio
21) Answer: B) "Reasonable Doubt"

22. Finish this lyric from Brandy and Monica's 1998 duet "The Boy Is Mine": "You need to give it up..."
- A) Had about enough
- B) Stop playing games
- C) I'm not gonna fight

23. Who sang the chorus on Mase's 1997 hit "Feel So Good"?
- A) Kelly Price
- B) Faith Evans
- C) 112

24. Which hip hop group released the song "California Love" in 1995?
- A) N.W.A.
- B) Cypress Hill
- C) 2Pac and Dr. Dre

22) Answer: A) Had about enough
23) Answer: A) Kelly Price
24) Answer: C) 2Pac and Dr. Dre

25. What was the title of Missy Elliott's debut album released in 1997?
   A) "Supa Dupa Fly"
   B) "Da Real World"
   C) "Miss E... So Addictive"

26. Who was Pepa's witness in the 1993 hit "Shoop"?
   A) Her Mom
   B) Her Niece
   C) Her Girl

27. Which R&B group released the song "If I Ever Fall in Love" in 1992?
   A) Jodeci
   B) Shai
   C) Dru Hill

25) Answer: A) "Supa Dupa Fly"
26) Answer: B) Her niece
27) Answer: B) Shai

28. Who released the album "The Velvet Rope" in 1997?
   A) Janet Jackson
   B) Toni Braxton
   C) Aaliyah

29. Finish this lyric from Bone Thugs-N-Harmony's 1995 hit "Tha Crossroads": "Livin' in a hateful world sendin' me straight to..."
   A) sendin' me straight to home
   B) sendin' me straight to heaven
   C) sendin' me straight to hell

30. What was the title of Mariah Carey's 1997 album?
   A) "Daydream"
   B) "Butterfly"
   C) "Music Box"

28) Answer: A) Janet Jackson
29) Answer: B) sendin' me straight to heaven
30) Answer: B) "Butterfly"

31. Which artist released the album "Share My World" in 1997?
   A) Mary J. Blige
   B) Erykah Badu
   C) Faith Evans

32. Who released the hit single "I Will Always Love You" in 1992?
   A) Toni Braxton
   B) Whitney Houston
   C) Mariah Carey

33. Finish this lyric from OutKast's 1998 hit "Rosa Parks": "Ah ha, hush that fuss..."
   A) Everybody move to the back of the bus
   B) Ain't nobody 'round here playin' with us
   C) Act like you never seen a crew like us

31) Answer: A) Mary J. Blige
32) Answer: B) Whitney Houston
33) Answer: A) Everybody move to the back of the bus

34. What was the title of Ginuwine's debut album released in 1996?
   A) "100% Ginuwine"
   B) "The Life"
   C) "Ginuwine...The Bachelor"

35. Who released the album "Mama's Gun" in 2000?
   A) Alicia Keys
   B) Lauryn Hill
   C) Erykah Badu

36. Finish this lyric from the hit 1993 song "Bump n' Grind": "You say he's not treating you right…"
   A) Let me hold you tight
   B) Lady spend the night
   C) Lets make love all night

34) Answer: C) "Ginuwine...The Bachelor"
35) Answer: C) Erykah Badu
36) Answer: B) Lady spend the night

37. Finish the lyric from Jon B's 1997 hit "They don't know": "Don't listen to what people say…"
   A) they don't know what they're talking about
   B) they don't know about you and me
   C) that's just jealousy


38. Finish this lyric from Sisqo's 1999 hit "Thong Song": "She had dumps like a truck…"
   A) Thighs like what
   B) Hips like what
   C) Back like what


39. Who released the album "Supernatural" in 1999?
   A) Santana
   B) Enrique Iglesias
   C) Ricky Martin


37) Answer: B) they don't know about you and me
38) Answer: A) Thighs like what
39) Answer: A) Santana

40. Which hip hop artist released the song "Juicy" in 1994?
   A) Nas
   B) LL Cool J
   C) The Notorious B.I.G.

41. What group won "Best new rap group" at the 1995 Source awards?
   A) Luniz
   B) OutKast
   C) Naughty by Nature

42. Finish this lyric from TLC's 1992 hit "Ain't 2 Proud 2 Beg": "Thinkin' short of what you got..."
   A) And I'm lookin hot to trot
   B) Better get it while it's hot
   C) And the lovin don't stop

40) Answer: C) The Notorious B.I.G.
41) Answer: B) OutKast
42) Answer: B) Better get it while it's hot

43. What was the chart toping hit single from TLC's 1999 album "FanMail"?
    A) Waterfalls
    B) No Scrubs
    C) Creep

44. Which hip hop group released the song "Jump Around" in 1992?
    A) Cypress Hill
    B) House of Pain
    C) Beastie Boys

45. What was the title of Toni Braxton's debut album released in 1993?
    A) "Secrets"
    B) "The Heat"
    C) "Toni Braxton"

43) Answer: B) No Scrubs
44) Answer: B) House of Pain
45) Answer: C) "Toni Braxton"

46. Finish this lyric from 2Pac's 1995 hit "Dear Mama": "And I could see you comin' home after work late..."
    A) help me with my tie before a hot date.
    B) You're in the kitchen, tryin' to fix us a hotplate.
    C) tears run down your eye due to our sad fate.

47. Who sang the chorus on Coolio's 1995 hit "Gangsta's Paradise"?
    A) Nate Dogg
    B) Gerald Levert
    C) L.V.

48. Who released the song "Pony" in 1996?
    A) Jagged Edge
    B) Next
    C) Ginuwine

46) Answer: C) You're in the kitchen, tryin' to fix us a hotplate.
47) Answer: C) L.V.
48) Answer: C) Ginuwine

49. What was the title of OutKast's debut album released in 1994?
   A) "Aquemini"
   B) "Speakerboxxx/The Love Below"
   C) "Southernplayalisticadillacmuzik"


50. Finish this lyric from Brandy's 1998 hit "Have You Ever?": "Have you ever loved somebody so much..."
   A) It makes you cry
   B) You can't sleep at night
   C) It hurts inside


51. Who released the album "The Don Killuminati: The 7 Day Theory" in 1996?
   A) 2Pac
   B) Nas
   C) Jay-Z

49) Answer: C) "Southernplayalisticadillacmuzik"
50) Answer: A) It makes you cry
51) Answer: A) 2Pac

52. Which hip hop artist released the song "It Was a Good Day" in 1993?

   A) Ice Cube
   B) Snoop Dogg
   C) LL Cool J

53. What was the title of Boyz II Men's debut album released in 1991?

   A) "Cooleyhighharmony"
   B) "II"
   C) "Evolution"

54. Finish this lyric from Aaliyah's 1996 hit "If Your Girl Only Knew": "She would probably leave you alone ..."

   A) She would probably trash your house when nobodies home
   B) She would probably call ya boys number out yo phone
   C) She would probably curse you out and unplug her phone.

52) Answer: A) Ice Cube
53) Answer: A) "Cooleyhighharmony"
54) Answer: C) She would probably curse you out and unplug her phone

55. Who released the album "Rhythm Nation 1814" in 1989?
   A) Janet Jackson
   B) Mariah Carey
   C) Whitney Houston

56. Which R&B group released the song "Creep" in 1994?
   A) Destiny's Child
   B) En Vogue
   C) TLC

57. What was the title of Snoop Dogg's debut album released in 1993?
   A) "Doggystyle"
   B) "Tha Doggfather"
   C) "The Chronic"

55) Answer: A) Janet Jackson
56) Answer: C) TLC
57) Answer: A) "Doggystyle"

58. Finish this lyric from TLC's 1999 hit "No Scrubs": "A scrub is a guy that..."
   A) Can't get no love from me
   B) Ain't got no time for me
   C) Can't buy me what I need

59. Who sang the hook on Nelly's 2002 hit "Hot in Herre"?
   A) Dani Stevenson
   B) Kelly Rowland
   C) Christina Aguilera

60. Which hip hop artist released the album "Da Real World" in 1999?
   A) Missy Elliott
   B) Eve
   C) Fat Joe

58) Answer: A) Can't get no love from me
59) Answer: A) Dani Stevenson
60) Answer: A) Missy Elliott

61. What was the title of TLC's debut album released in 1992?
    A) "CrazySexyCool"
    B) "FanMail"
    C) "Oooooooohhh... On the TLC Tip"

62. Finish this lyric from Sisqo's 2000 hit "Incomplete": "Even though it seems I have everything..."
    A) It's nothing if i don't have you
    B) I don't want to be a lonely fool
    C) If i lost you i'd be a damn fool

63. Name this single from Dru Hill's album "Dru World Order" in 2002?
    A) In my bed
    B) I Should Be
    C) 5 steps

63) Answer: B) I Should Be
62) Answer: B) I don't want to be a lonely fool
61) Answer: C) "Oooooooohhh... On the TLC Tip"

64. Which R&B group released the song "No, No, No" in 1997?
   A) Destiny's Child
   B) 702
   C) Xscape

65. What was the title of Jay-Z's album released in 2001?
   A) "The Blueprint"
   B) "Vol. 2... Hard Knock Life"
   C) "The Black Album"

66. Finish this lyric from Missy Elliott's 2002 hit "Work It": "Gimme all your numbers so I can phone ya..."
   A) Your girl acting stank then call me over
   B) Money in the bank is all i want ya
   C) Call me late night so i come over

64) Answer: A) Destiny's Child
65) Answer: A) "The Blueprint"
66) Answer: A) Your girl acting stank then call me over

67. Who released the album "Country Grammar" in 2000?
   A) Nelly
   B) Ludacris
   C) Ja Rule

68. Which hip hop artist released the song "Get Ur Freak On" in 2001?
   A) Lil' Kim
   B) Missy Elliott
   C) Eve

69. What was the title of Usher's album released in 2004?
   A) "Confessions"
   B) "8701"
   C) "My Way"

67) Answer: A) Nelly
68) Answer: B) Missy Elliott
69) Answer: A) "Confessions"

70. Finish this lyric from Alicia Keys' 2001 hit "Fallin'": "Sometimes I feel good..."
    A) Sometimes I feel blue
    B) At times I feel used
    C) At times I feel you

71. Who sang the hook on Ja Rule's 2001 hit "Always on Time"?
    A) Ashanti
    B) Christina Milian
    C) Mya

72. Which R&B group released the song "Waterfalls" in 1995?
    A) TLC
    B) En Vogue
    C) Destiny's Child

70) Answer: B) At times I feel used
71) Answer: A) Ashanti
72) Answer: A) TLC

73. In Nelly's 2000 hit song E.I. what was he a sucker for?
   A) Apple Bottom jeans and boots with the fur
   B) Corn rows and manicured toes
   C) Baby Phat jeans and Secret Vickie's

74. Finish this lyric from Ashanti's 2002 hit "Foolish": "See, my days are cold without you..."
   A) But I'm hurting while I'm with you
   B) But I don't know why i'm with you
   C) But I'm learning why i'm with you

75. Who released the album "The College Dropout" in 2004?
   A) Kanye West
   B) 50 Cent
   C) Eminem

73) Answer: C) Corn rows and manicured toes
74) Answer: A) But I'm hurting while I'm with you
75) Answer: A) Kanye West

76. Which hip hop artist released the song "In Da Club" in 2003?
   A) 50 Cent
   B) Jay-Z
   C) Nas

77. What was the title of OutKast's album released in 2003?
   A) "Aquemini"
   B) "Speakerboxxx/The Love Below"
   C) "Stankonia"

78. Finish this lyric from Usher's 2004 hit "Yeah!": "Conversation got heavy..."
   A) She was telling me she's ready to go
   B) She had me feeling like she's ready to blow
   C) She was telling me she's ready for more

76) Answer: A) 50 Cent
77) Answer: B) "Speakerboxxx/The Love Below"
78) Answer: B) She had me feeling like she's ready to blow

79. Who released the album "Dangerously in Love" in 2003?
   A) Beyoncé
   B) Jennifer Lopez
   C) Ashanti

80. Which R&B group released the song "Your Letter" in 1998?
   A) 112
   B) Jagged Edge
   C) Next

81. What was the title of Alicia Keys' debut album released in 2001?
   A) "The Diary of Alicia Keys"
   B) "Songs in A Minor"
   C) "As I Am"

79) Answer: A) Beyoncé
80) Answer: A) 112
81) Answer: B) "Songs in A Minor"

82. Finish this lyric from Usher's 2001 hit "U Remind Me": "You remind me of a..."
    A) Love I once knew
    B) Girl that I once knew
    C) Love that wasn't true

83. Who sang the chorus on Ja Rule's 2001 hit "Put It on Me"?
    A) Ashanti
    B) Lil Mo
    C) Jennifer Lopez

84. Which hip hop artist released the song "Gold Digger" in 2005?
    A) Kanye West
    B) Jamie Foxx
    C) Jay-Z

82) Answer: B) Girl that I once knew
83) Answer: B) Lil Mo
84) Answer: A) Kanye West

85. What was the title of Mary J. Blige's album released in 1994?
   A) "My Life"
   B) "What's the 411?"
   C) "Share My World"

86. Finish this lyric from Nelly's 2002 hit "Hot in Herre": "It's gettin' hot in here..."
   A) So take off all your clothes
   B) Let's turn up the stereo
   C) We're partying all night long

87. Who released the album "The Emancipation of Mimi" in 2005?
   A) Mariah Carey
   B) Christina Aguilera
   C) Whitney Houston

85) Answer: A) "My Life"
86) Answer: A) So take off all your clothes
87) Answer: A) Mariah Carey

88. Which R&B group released the song "Say My Name" in 1999?
   A) Destiny's Child
   B) En Vogue
   C) TLC

89. What was the title of Ashanti's debut album released in 2002?
   A) "Chapter II"
   B) "Concrete Rose"
   C) "Ashanti"

90. Finish this lyric from Kanye West's 2005 hit "Gold Digger": "Far as girls you got…"
   A) A lot
   B) A flock
   C) A line around the block

Answer: A) Destiny's Child
Answer: C) "Ashanti"
Answer: B) A flock

91. Finish this lyric from Ushers 2004 song "Confessions Part II": " The first thing that came to mind was you…"

   A) Second thing was is this a lie or is it true
   B) Second thing was how am i going to tell you
   C) Second thing was how do I know if it's mine and is it true


92. Which hip hop artist released the song "Lose Yourself" in 2002?
   A) Eminem
   B) 50 Cent
   C) Jay-Z


93. What was the title of OutKast's album released in 2000?
   A) "Stankonia"
   B) "Aquemini"
   C) "Speakerboxxx/The Love Below"


Answer: A) Second thing was how do I know if it's mine and is it true
Answer: A) Eminem
Answer: A) "Stankonia"

94. Finish this lyric from Alicia Keys' 2003 hit "If I Ain't Got You": "Some people want it all..."
    A) But I don't want nothing at all
    B) But I don't want nothing baby
    C) But I don't want nothing else

95. Who sang the hook on Nelly's 2004 hit "Over and Over"?
    A) Christina Aguilera
    B) Kelly Rowland
    C) Tim McGraw

96. Which R&B group released the song "No More (Baby I'ma Do Right)" in 2000?
    A) 3LW
    B) TLC
    C) Destiny's Child

94) Answer: A) But I don't want nothing at all
95) Answer: C) Tim McGraw
96) Answer: A) 3LW

97. In Kanye West's 2004 song "Spaceship" where did he work?
    A) Louis Vuitton
    B) Jack in the Box
    C) Gap


98. Finish this lyric from Usher's 2004 hit "Burn": "When your feeling ain't the same..."
    A) And your body don't want to
    B) And your heart don't want to
    C) And your love don't seem to


99. Who released the album "Good Girl Gone Bad" in 2007?
    A) Rihanna
    B) Beyoncé
    C) Alicia Keys

97) Answer: C) Gap
98) Answer: A) And your body don't want to
99) Answer: A) Rihanna

100. Which artist released the song "Hollaback Girl" in 2005?
   A) Fergie
   B) Gwen Stefani
   C) Christina Aguilera

101. Which rapper was featured on Jon B's 1998 song "Are you still down"?
   A) Snoop Dogg
   B) 2Pac
   C) Jay-Z

102. Finish this lyric from Missy Elliott's 2001 hit "Get Ur Freak On": "Missy be puttin' it down..."
   A) I'm the hottest in town
   B) y'all can't stop me now
   C) I'm the hottest 'round

100) Answer: B) Gwen Stefani
101) Answer: B) 2Pac
102) Answer: C) I'm the hottest 'round

103. Who sang the chorus on Kanye West's 2005 hit "Slow Jamz"?
  A) Ashanti
  B) Keyshia Cole
  C) Jamie Fox

104. Which R&B group released the song "Unpretty" in 1999?
  A) TLC
  B) Destiny's Child
  C) En Vogue

105. What was the title of Usher's album released in 2008?
  A) "Here I Stand"
  B) "Confessions"
  C) "8701"

103) Answer: C) Jamie Foxx
104) Answer: A) TLC
105) Answer: A) "Here I Stand"

106. Finish this lyric from Nelly's 2000 hit "Ride wit Me": "We 3-wheeling in the fo' with…"
   A) The oldies
   B) The gold D's
   C) The 40's

107. Who released the album "CrazySexyCool" in 1994?
   A) TLC
   B) Destiny's Child
   C) En Vogue

108. Which hip hop artist released the song "Hot Boyz" in 1999?
   A) Missy Elliott
   B) Lil' Kim
   C) Foxy Brown

106) Answer: B) The gold D's
107) Answer: A) TLC
108) Answer: A) Missy Elliott

109. What was the title of Mariah Carey's debut album released in 1990?
   A) "Butterfly"
   B) "Daydream"
   C) "Mariah Carey"


110. Finish this lyric from Ja Rule's 2001 hit "Livin' It Up": "Probably treat this chick..."
   A) More better
   B) To dinner
   C) however


111. Who rapped along side Usher in his 2004 hit "Yeah!"?
   A) Nelly
   B) Ludacris
   C) Lil Jon

109) Answer: C) "Mariah Carey"
110) Answer: A) More better
111) Answer: B) Ludacris

112. Which R&B group released the song "Weak" in 1993?
   A) Xscape
   B) SWV
   C) 702

113. What was the title of Eminem's album released in 2000?
   A) "The Slim Shady LP"
   B) "The Marshall Mathers LP"
   C) "Encore"

114. Finish this lyric from TLC's 1992 hit "Ain't 2 Proud 2 Beg": "If I need it in the mornin'..."
   A) Or in the middle of the night
   B) Or when the time is feeling's right
   C) Or when I'm by your side

112) Answer: B) SWV
113) Answer: B) "The Marshall Mathers LP"
114) Answer: A) Or in the middle of the night

115. Who released the album "Back to Black" in 2006?
   A) Amy Winehouse
   B) Adele
   C) Duffy


116. Which hip hop artist released the song "Stand Up" in 2003?
   A) Ludacris
   B) Nelly
   C) T.I.


117. What was the hit single from Destiny's Child debut album released in 1998?
   A) "Bills, Bills, Bills"
   B) "No, No, No,"
   C) "Survivor"

115) Answer: A) Amy Winehouse
116) Answer: A) Ludacris
117) Answer: B) "No, No, No,"

118. Finish this lyric from Usher's 1997 hit "You Make Me Wanna...": "Before anything began between us..."
- A) You were my boy's girlfriend
- B) You were like my best friend
- C) We started off as best friends

119. Who sang the chorus on Nelly's 2002 hit "Dilemma"?
- A) Ashanti
- B) Kelly Rowland
- C) Christina Aguilera

120. Which R&B group released the song "Bills, Bills, Bills" in 1999?
- A) Destiny's Child
- B) En Vogue
- C) TLC

118) Answer: B) You were like my best friend
119) Answer: B) Kelly Rowland
120) Answer: A) Destiny's Child

121. Who sang the hook on Jay-Z's 1998 song "Can't Knock the Hustle"?
   A) Foxy Brown
   B) Missy Elliott
   C) Mary J. Blige


122. Finish this Ludacris lyric from Missy Elliott's 2001 hit "One Minute Man": "It's time to set your clock back 'bout as long as you can i stop daylight, it's Ludacris, the..."
   A) One minute man
   B) Maintenance man
   C) Handyman


123. In OutKast's 2003 song "Roses" what did Andre 3000 say they smelled like?
   A) Shampoo
   B) Fondue
   C) Boo boo


121) Answer: C) Mary J. Blige
122) Answer: B) Maintenance man
123) Answer: C) Boo boo

124. Which hip hop artist released the song "Gin and Juice" in 1993?
   A) Snoop Dogg
   B) Dr. Dre
   C) Ice Cube

125. What was the title of Alicia Keys' album released in 2007?
   A) "As I Am"
   B) "The Element of Freedom"
   C) "Songs in A Minor"

126. Finish this lyric from Nelly's 2002 hit "Air Force Ones": "I said give me two pairs..."
   A) I need two pairs
   B) So I can get to stompin'
   C) So I can get to jumpin'

124) Answer: A) Snoop Dogg
125) Answer: A) "As I Am"
126) Answer: A) I need two pairs

127. Who released the album "It's Dark and Hell Is Hot" in 1998?
   A) DMX
   B) Nas
   C) Jay-Z

128. Which R&B group released the song "Don't Let Go (Love)" in 1996?
   A) En Vogue
   B) SWV
   C) 702

129. Finish this lyric from Janet Jackson's 1993 hit "Any Time, Any Place": "I don't wanna stop just because people walking by…"
   A) Mocking us
   B) Are watching us
   C) starting a fuss

127) Answer: A) DMX
128) Answer: A) En Vogue
129) Answer: B) Are watching us

130. What was the title of Jay-Z's album released in 2003?
   A) "The Blueprint"
   B) "Reasonable Doubt"
   C) "The Black Album"

131. Finish this Jeezy lyric from Usher's 2008 hit "Love in This Club": "You ever made love to a thug in the club with…"
   A) The lights on
   B) His ice on
   C) The mic on

132. Which hip hop artist released the song "Hot in Herre" in 2002?
   A) Nelly
   B) Ja Rule
   C) T.I.

130) Answer: C) "The Black Album"
131) Answer: B) His ice on
132) Answer: A) Nelly

133. "Creep", "Waterfalls" and "Red Light Special" are all hits from what TLC album?

   A) "FanMail"
   B) "CrazySexyCool"
   C) "Oooooooohhh... On the TLC Tip"


134. Finish this Ludacris lyric from Usher's 2004 hit "Yeah!": "Watch out, my outfit's ridiculous In the club..."

   A) lookin' so meticulous
   B) lookin' so conspicuous
   C) lookin' so promiscuous


135. "The Diary of Alicia Keys" was released in what year?

   A) 2003
   B) 1999
   C) 2001


133) Answer: B) "CrazySexyCool"
134) Answer: B) lookin' so conspicuous
135) Answer: A) 2003

136. Three 6 Mafia Won an Oscar for what song in 2006?
   A) "Sippin On Some Syrup"
   B) "It's Hard Out Here for a Pimp"
   C) "Stay Fly"

137. This Geto Boys song was featured in the 1999 cult classic movie Office Space?
   A) "G code"
   B) "Mind playing tricks on me"
   C) "Damn it feels good to be a gangsta"

138. Finish this lyric from Missy Elliott's 2002 hit "Work It": "I put my thing down, flip it and..."
   A) Reverse it
   B) Turn it around
   C) Shake it up

136) Answer: B) "It's Hard Out Here for a Pimp"
137) Answer: C) "Damn it feels good to be a gangsta"
138) Answer: A) Reverse it

139. What year did Nelly's hit "Ride wit Me" debut
   A) 2000
   B) 1998
   C) 2003

140. Which hip hop artist released the song "Empire State of Mind" in 2009?
   A) Jay-Z
   B) Kanye West
   C) Drake

141. What was the title of Destiny's Child's album released in 1999?
   A) "Destiny's Child"
   B) "The Writing's on the Wall"
   C) "Survivor"

139) Answer: A) 2000
140) Answer: A) Jay-Z
141) Answer: B) "The Writing's on the Wall"

142. Finish this lyric from Usher's 1997 hit "Nice & Slow": "It's seven o' clock on the dot. I'm in my drop top..."
   A) Fallin asleep
   B) Looking for you
   C) Cruisin' the streets

143. Rapper 2 Short is from what California city?
   A) San Francisco
   B) Oakland
   C) San Diego

144. Who Rapped the hit "Fantastic Voyage" released in 1994?
   A) LL Cool J
   B) Coolio
   C) Snoop Dogg

142) Answer: C) Cruisin' the streets
143) Answer: B) Oakland
144) Answer: B) Coolio

145. What is Master P's government name?
   A) Patrick Houston
   B) Calvin Broadus
   C) Percy Miller

146. Finish this lyric from Missy Elliott's 2002 hit "Get Ur Freak On": "Me and Timbaland been..."
   A) Out since before you know
   B) Hot since twenty years ago
   C) Doing this since way back you know

147. Finish this lyric from Tevin Campbell's 1993 hit "Can we talk": "Next time you come my way…"
   A) i won't know what to say
   B) I'll know just what to say
   C) I'll run the other way

145) Answer: C) Percy Miller
146) Answer: B) Hot since twenty years ago
147) Answer: B) I'll know just what to say

148. What is rapper Calvin Broadus's stage name?
   A) 50 Cent
   B) Snoop Dogg
   C) T.I.


149. Finish this lyric from T-Pain's hit "I'm sprung":
" Dog she got me, Got me doin' things…"
   A) she like to do
   B) I'd never do
   C) she want to do


150. Finish this lyric from Nelly's 2004 hit "Hot in Herre": "I got a friend with a pole..."
   A) In the basement
   B) In the bedroom
   C) In the dance club

148) Answer: B) Snoop Dogg
149) Answer: B) I'd never do
150) Answer: A) In the basement

151. Who released the album "Tha Carter III" in 2008?
   A) Lil Wayne
   B) Drake
   C) Kanye West

152. Who released the R&B hit song "No Nobody" in 1996?
   A) TLC
   B) Keith Sweat
   C) En Vogue

153. Name Jodeci's debut album release in 1991?
   A) "Love always"
   B) "The Velvet Rope"
   C) "Forever My Lady"

151) Answer: A) Lil Wayne
152) Answer: B) Keith Sweat
153) Answer: C) "Forever My Lady"

154. What is Ja Rule's government name?
   A) Jeffrey Atkins
   B) Jermaine Cole
   C) Jeffrey Townes

155. In what City and State was the R&B group Color Me Badd formed?
   A) New York, NY
   B) Oklahoma City, OK
   C) Miami, FL

156. Which artist released the song " Big Pimpin'" in 2000?
   A) Jay-Z
   B) Snoop Dogg
   C) Dr. Dre

154) Answer: A) Jeffrey Atkins
155) Answer: B) Oklahoma City, OK
156) Answer: A) Jay-Z

157. Finish this lyric from Color Me Badd's 1991 hit "I wanna sex you up": "come inside take off your coat…"
- A) I'll make you nice and warm
- B) I'll make you feel at home
- C) And we're all alone

158. Referring to the R&B group what does the acronym S.W.V stand for?
- A) Singing with Vanity
- B) Singing with Virtue
- C) Sisters with Voices

159. Who released the album "Good Girl Gone Bad" in 2007?
- A) Rihanna
- B) Beyoncé
- C) Alicia Keys

157) Answer: B) I'll make you feel at home
158) Answer: C) Sisters with Voices
159) Answer: A) Rihanna

160. Finish this lyric from Gwen Stefani's 2004 hit "Hollaback Girl": "A few times I've been around that track…"
    A) and it always happens just like that
    B) So it's not just gonna happen like that
    C) and i don't know it keeps pulling me back


161. What does the 'J' stand for in singer Mary J. Blige's name?
    A) Jill
    B) Jane
    C) Josephine


162. Finish this lyric from Missy Elliott's 1997 hit "The Rain": "Beep, beep, who got the keys..."
    A) to my fleet
    B) to my Beemer
    C) to the Jeep


160) Answer: B) So it's not just gonna happen like that
161) Answer: B) Jane
162) Answer: C) to the Jeep

163. Who rapped along side Kanye West in his 2005 hit "Slow Jamz"?
   A) Ashanti
   B) Keyshia Cole
   C) Twista

164. What is Artist Faheem Najm stage name?
   A) Common
   B) T-Pain
   C) Mos Def

165. The Rap duo Big Tymers was made up of which artists?
   A) Prodigy and Havoc
   B) Mannie Fresh and Birdman
   C) Malice and Pusha T

163) Answer: C) Twista
164) Answer: B) T-Pain
165) Answer: B) Mannie Fresh and Birdman

166. Finish this lyric from Nelly's 2000 hit "Ride wit Me": "Oh why do I live this way? Hey..."
    A) we do it for the honeys
    B) I love it when its sunny
    C) must be the money


167. In what city and state was the group TLC formed?
    A) Houston, TX
    B) Atlanta, GA
    C) Detroit, MI


168. Which hip hop artist released the song "Hot Boyz" in 1999?
    A) Missy Elliott
    B) Lil' Wayne
    C) Foxy Brown


166) Answer: C) must be the money
167) Answer: B) Atlanta, GA
168) Answer: A) Missy Elliott

169. Finish this lyric from K. P. & Envyi 1998 Jam "Swing My Way": " shorty swing my way…"
   A) and come dance on me
   B) sho look good to me
   C) and come talk to me


170. Name the 1995 summer time hit by Ghost Town DJ's
   A) "In a dream"
   B) "My Boo"
   C) "C'Mon n' Ride It"


171. What is Rapper DMX's government name?
   A) Earl Simmons
   B) Calvin Broadus
   C) O'Shea Jackson

169) Answer: B) sho look good to me
170) Answer: B) "My Boo"
171) Answer: A) Earl Simmons

172. Which R&B group released the song "No Diggity" in 1996?
   A) Blackstreet
   B) Boyz II Men
   C) Jodeci

173. Finish this lyric from Erykah Badu's hit " on and on": " I think I need a cup of tea…"
   A) The world keeps turning
   B) my throat is burnin'
   C) The world keeps burnin'

174. What is Nelly's government name?
   A) Nelson Jackson
   B) Cornell Haynes
   C) Nicolas Anderson

172) Answer: A) Blackstreet
173) Answer: C) The world keeps burnin'
174) Answer: B) Cornell Haynes

175. Who released the album "The Blueprint" in 2001?
    A) Jay-Z
    B) Nas
    C) DMX

176. Which hip hop artist released the song "California Love" in 1996?
    A) Ice Cube
    B) Snoop Dogg
    C) 2Pac

177. What was the title of Destiny's Child's album released in 2001?
    A) "Destiny's Child"
    B) "The Writing's on the Wall"
    C) "Survivor"

175) Answer: A) Jay-Z
176) Answer: C) 2Pac
177) Answer: C) "Survivor"

178. Finish this lyric from Hi Five's 1990 hit " I like the way ( kissing game)": " we've got it good, we have it all it seems…"
   A) your all I need
   B) we're living dream
   C) I see you in my dreams

179. Who released the album "Supa Dupa Fly" in 1997?
   A) Missy Elliott
   B) Lil' Kim
   C) Foxy Brown

180. Which R&B group released the song "Water Runs Dry" in 1995?
   A) Boyz II Men
   B) Jodeci
   C) 112

178) Answer: B) we're living dream
179) Answer: A) Missy Elliott
180) Answer: A) Boyz II Men

181. Finish this lyric from Ja Rule's 2002 hit "Always on Time": "And I gave you my all, now baby..."
   A) Be mine
   B) It's time
   C) I'm fine

181) Answer: A) Be mine

Congratulations! You've reached the end of this captivating journey through the world of 90s - 00's hip hop and R&B. We hope this trivia book has rekindled fond memories, sparked new interests, and shed light on the immense impact of this era. The 90s - 00's were a time of artistic innovation, cultural shifts, and groundbreaking music that continues to resonate with fans around the world.

The influence of this era in hip hop and R&B can still be felt today, as artists and producers draw inspiration from this golden era. Its impact extends beyond music, shaping fashion, language, and popular culture as a whole. From the introspective rhymes of Nas to the sultry vocals of Mary J. Blige, the era produced timeless classics that continue to inspire and move audiences across generations.

We hope this trivia book has deepened your appreciation for the artists who paved the way and the cultural revolution they ignited. Whether you aced every question or discovered new gems along the way, we encourage you to keep exploring the rich tapestry of hip hop and R&B. Let the music take you on a journey, and let the spirit of the old school live on in your heart.

Thank you for joining us on this trip down memory lane, and remember, the beat never stops.

Printed in Great Britain
by Amazon